Llewod Pont Britannia
The Lions of Britannia Bridge

Ysgrifenwyd gan yr awdur dawnus F.J. Beerling
Dylunwyd y llyfr gan Lucy Gilbert
Printiwyd ar Ynys Môn, Cymru gan WO Jones
Cyhoeddwyd gan Ymddiriedolaeth Treftadaeth Menai, Dyddiad cyhoeddi Rhagfyr 2020
Hawlfraint © Ymddiriedolaeth Treftadaeth Gymunedol Porthaethwy
Cedwir pob hawl
ISBN: 978-0-9932351-4-6

Written by accomplished children's author F.J. Beerling
Book design by Lucy Gilbert
Printed on the Isle of Anglesey, Wales, by WO Jones
Published by Menai Heritage, Release date December 2020
Copyright © Menai Bridge Community Heritage Trust
All rights reserved.
ISBN: 978-0-9932351-4-6

Cefnogir gyda balchder gan Mott MacDonald
ymgynghorwyr peirianyddol, rheolaeth a datblygiad, byd-eang

Proudly sponsored by Mott MacDonald
a global engineering, management and development consultancy

Ni chaniateir atgynhyrchu unrhyw ran o'r cyhoeddiad hwn na'i gadw mewn cyfundrefn adferadwy, na'i drosglwyddo mewn unrhyw ddull na thrwy unrhyw gyfrwng electronig, tâp magnetig, mecanyddol, ffotocopio, recordio, nac fel arall heb ganiatâd ymlaen llaw gan y cyhoeddwyr.
Mae F.J. Beerling yn mynnu'r hawl i gael ei chydnabod fel awdur y gwaith hwn yn unol â'r Ddeddf "Copyright, Designs & Patents "1988.
Mae Lucy Gilbert yn mynnu'r hawl i gael ei chydnabod fel darlunydd y gwaith hwn yn unol â'r Ddeddf "Copyright, Designs & Patents" 1988.
Defnyddiwyd penrhyddid artistig wrth baratoi'r llyfr hwn. Er mwyn cael gwybodaeth technegol a hanesyddol mwy manwl gellir mynd i menaibridges.co.uk/education

Er bod pob gofal wedi ei gymeryd wrth baratoi'r llyfr hwn, nid yw'r cyhoeddwr, awdur, na'r darlunydd yn derbyn unrhyw gyfrifoldeb am gamgymeriadau neu hepgoriadau. Ni dderbynir unrhyw gyfrifoldeb chwaith am gais am iawndal sy'n dilyn o ddefnyddio unrhyw wybodaeth â gynhwysir.

No part of this book shall be reproduced, stored in a retrieval system or transmitted in any form or by any means, electronic or mechanical, including photocopying, recording or by any information retrieval system without prior written permission of the publisher.
F.J. Beerling asserts the right to be identified as the author of this work in accordance with the Copyright, Designs & Patents Act 1988.
Lucy Gilbert asserts the right to be identified as the illustrator of this work in accordance with the Copyright, Designs & Patents Act 1988.
Artistic license has been used in the telling of this story and its illustrations. For more detailed technical and historical information go to menaibridges.co.uk/education

Although every precaution has been taken in the preparation of this book, the publisher, author and illustrator assume no responsibility for errors or omissions. Neither is any liability assumed for damages resulting from the use of this information herein.

Mae'r llyfr hwn wedi ei gyflwyno i'r holl blant fydd yn beiriannwyr y dyfodol.
Diolchwn i'r canlynol:
Jenny Porter am y syniad gwreiddiol,
Gareth E. Jones am y cyfieithiad i'r Gymraeg
a holl wirfoddolwyr Treftadaeth Menai sydd wedi cyfranu o'u gwybodaeth hanesyddol a pheirianyddol.

This book is dedicated to all those children who will be the engineers of the future.
Our thanks to the following:
Jenny Porter for the initial idea,
Gareth E. Jones for his translation
and the many Menai Heritage volunteers
who have contributed their historical and engineering expert knowledge.

Mae Treftadaeth Menai yn fudiad cymunedol sy'n rhedeg amgueddfa sy'n dathlu a dehongli treftadaeth y Fenai, ei phontydd a'r ardal o'i chwmpas. Croesawn ymwelwyr yn ogystal â gwirfoddolwyr a chyfranwyr sy'n dymuno'n helpu yn ein gwaith.
Menai Heritage is a community organisation that runs a museum celebrating and
interpreting the heritage of the Menai Strait, its bridges and the surrounding area.
We welcome visitors as well as volunteers and contributors who wish to help us in this work.

Canolfan Thomas Telford Centre
Ffordd Mona Road
Porthaethwy / Menai Bridge
Ynys Môn / Isle of Anglesey, LL59 5EA
menaibridges.co.uk

Roedd Uarda yn blentyn 9 oed ac yn eithaf clyfar. Roedd hi'n dda am ddatrys problemau a phosau. Roedd hi hefyd â diddordeb mawr mewn sut oedd pethau'n gweithio…

…felly, pan ddaeth y cyfle iddi astudio gwyddoniaeth, technoleg, peirianneg a mathemateg yn yr ysgol roedd Uarda wrth ei bodd.

Buasai astudio'r rhain yn ei galluogi i wireddu ei breuddwyd o fod yn beiriannydd ar ôl tyfu fyny.

Heddiw yr oedd am i'w thad fynd â hi dros Bont Britannia sy'n croesi'r Fenai yng Ngogledd Cymru. Mae pedwar llew carreg yn gwarchod y fynedfa trên ar bob ochor i'r Bont. Mae cledrau ar gyfer trenau a ffordd ar gyfer faniau, loriau a cheir…

…ond dim i'w car nhw, mi wnaeth dorri i lawr ar y ffordd yno.

Uarda was a clever 9-year old. She was good at problem solving and puzzles. She was also fascinated with how things worked…

…so, when her school introduced them to the science, technology, engineering, and maths curriculum, Uarda was over the moon.

The study of these would help Uarda achieve her dream - she wanted to become an engineer when she grew up.

Today, she wanted her dad to take her across the Britannia Bridge over the Menai Strait in Wales. It had four stone lions guarding the train entrance on either side of the Bridge. There was a rail track for trains and a road for vans, lorries, and cars…

…but not their car, on the way there it had broken down!

Wrth lwc, fe wyddai tad Uarda ddigon am beirianneg i drwsio'r car. Felly, fe'i gadawodd o'n potsian dan y bonet ac aeth am dro.
Roedd Uarda wedi rhyfeddu gyda Pont Britannia. Fe'i hadeiladwyd fel pont reilffordd ym 1850. Mae yn 460 medr o hyd ac yn 31 medr o uchder fel y gallai llongau hwyliau basio oddi tanni. Bu bron iddi gael ei difetha'n llwyr gan dân ym 1970 a bu rhaid ei hail gynllunio, gwnaethant adeiladu ffordd uwchben y rheilffordd yr un pryd…
…Dyna pryd y collwyd y llewod godidog.

Fortunately, Uarda's dad knew enough about mechanical engineering to fix the car. So, Uarda left him tinkering under the bonnet and went for a walk.
She was amazed by the Britannia Bridge. It had been built as a rail bridge in 1850. It was 460 metres long and 31 metres high so tall ships could pass under it until the bridge was almost destroyed by a fire in 1970, and it had to be re-designed, and then they built a road across the top of it…
…That was when the magnificent stone lions were lost.

…Hynny yw, eu colli o'r golwg gan eu bod wedi eu cuddio. Roeddynt yn dal i eistedd yn gwarchod mynedfa'r rheilffordd dros y Bont, ond pan adeiladwyd y dec ar gyfer ceir nid oedd modd i'w gweld o'r ffordd.

Ar ôl crwydro ychydig gwelodd Uarda un o'r llewod carreg ac agorodd ei cheg mewn syndod. Roedd yn anferth, roedd yn wych, mewn gwirionedd roedd yn 4 medr o uchder ac yn pwyso 30 tunnell.

"Sgwn'i sut es' ti i'r fan yna" meddai wrth ei hun wrth edrych ar y llew. Ond dyna'r llew yn siarad.

"Helo" meddai'r llew mewn llais dwfn er yn dyner. "Mae'n siŵr dy fod yn gofyn be ydw'i yn ei wneud yn y fan yma". Camodd Uarda'n ôl a bu bron iddi ddisgyn ar ei phen ôl. Roedd hi wedi syfrdanu, oedd y llew carreg wedi siarad efo hi?

…Lost from view that was, they were now hidden away. They still sat on guard at the rail entrance to the Britannia Bridge, but when the road deck was added they could not be seen from the road.

After a little walk Uarda found one of the stone lions and gasped. It was colossal, it was magnificent, it was in fact, nearly 4 metres tall and weighed 30 tonnes.

"I wonder how you got here," thought Uarda to herself looking up at the lion. Just then, the lion spoke.

"Hello," said the lion in a gentle but deep voice. "I bet you're wondering how I got here." Uarda took a step back and almost sat down on her bottom. She was in shock, had the stone lion just spoken to her?

Pwyllodd Uarda am funud i setlo'i nerfau. "Mi, mi, mi, mi, mi wyt ti'n gallu siarad!" meddai mewn rhyfeddod. "Medra'n wir", atebodd y llew gan wenu arni. "Rwyt ti'n anferth", meddai mewn ychydig gan obeithio nad oedd wedi pechu'r llew. "Ydwyf yn wir," atebodd y llew, "ond nid fi ydi'r unig un sydd yma, mae mwy ohonom ni".
Roedd Uarda yn gwybod fod yna bedwar llew carreg i gyd. Dau ar y tir mawr, ochor Bangor, a dau ar ochor Ynys Môn.
Roedd hi hefyd yn gwybod eu bod wedi eu cerfio allan o garreg galch leol gan gerflunydd o'r enw John Thomas.

Uarda steadied herself and her nerves and managed to speak. "You, you, you, you, you can talk?" she stammered. "I can indeed," replied the lion smiling down at her.
"You're colossal," she said after a while, hoping that the lion would not take offence. "I am indeed," replied the lion. "but I am not the only lion here, there are more of us."
Uarda knew that there were four stone lions in total. Two on the Bangor mainland side and two on the Anglesey side.
She also knew that they had been carved from local limestone and their sculptor was called John Thomas.

Roedd Uarda eisiau creu argraff dda ar y llew. Roedd hi wedi dysgu cymaint amdanynt yn y dosbarthiadau peirianneg a dyma hi, yn siarad efo un ohonynt.
"Mi wnes di ofyn sut cyrhaeddais i i'r fan yma," meddai'r llew."Wyt ti'n gwybod sut?"
Ysgwydodd Uarda'i phen mewn penbleth, mae hi'n hoffi posau ac yn hoffi datrys posau. Efallai y gallai ddatrys y pos yma hefyd.
Roedd yn rhaid iddi feddwl sut aeth y pedwar llew yna.

Uarda wanted to impress the lion. She had learnt so much about them in her engineering classes and here she was talking to one of them.
"You asked me how I got here," said the lion. "Do you know how?"
Uarda shook her head and looked puzzled, she likes puzzles, and she liked to solve them. Maybe she could solve this puzzle too.
She had to think about how the four stone lions had got there.

Dyma Uarda'n meddwl am ychydig ac yna dywedodd, "mae'n ddrwg gen'i, lle mae fy manars, f'enw i ydi Uarda sy'n cael ei ynganu fel Iw-ar-da, sut wyt ti."
Daliodd Uarda ei llaw allan fel ei bod am ysgwyd llaw efo'r llew.
"Toes gen'i ddim enw," meddai'r llew, "dim ond rhif, fi ydi llew Rhif Pedwar."
"Helo llew Rhif Pedwar" gwenodd Uarda.
"Helo Uarda," meddai'r llew. "Dyna enw anarferol!" "Ydi mae'o," meddai Uarda. "Mae fy nheulu'n dod o'r Aifft, a dweud y gwir rwyt ti'n edrych yn debyg i'r Sphinx o Giza yn yr Aifft ond fod gan hwnnw ben dyn ar gorff llew!"
Ychwanegodd y llew, "Pan gerfiwyd ni roedd pawb yn dweud ein bod yn anferth ac urddasol, yn union fel y Sphinx o'r Aifft."

Uarda thought for a while then said, "I'm sorry, where are my manners, my name is Uarda, it is pronounced, You-ar-da, how do you do."
Uarda held out her hand as if to shake the lion by its paw.
"I don't have a name," replied the lion, "only a number, I am lion number four."
"Hello lion number four" smiled Uarda.
"Hello Uarda," said the lion. "That's an unusual name? "Yes, it is," said Uarda. "My family come from Egypt. In fact, you look Egyptian too, you look a bit like the Great Sphinx of Giza except that has a human head on a lion's body!"
The lion added, "When we were carved, people said we were colossal and noble just like an Egyptian Sphinx."

Pendronodd Uarda am sut aeth y llewod i'w lle.
"Gefaist ti dy godi gan hofrennydd a'th ollwng yn dy le?" gofynnodd.
"Na" atebodd y llew.
"Gefaist ti dy gerfio allan o un darn mawr o garreg," gofynnodd Urada.
"Rhywbeth tebyg i hynny" atebodd y llew
"Gefaist ti dy gerfio yn agos i'r fan yma?" holodd Uarda gan wenu.
"Do," atebodd y llew," mewn gweithdy bach yr ochor isaf i'r Bont," ond ar hyn dyma Uarda yn torri ar ei draws…
…"ac wedyn fesul darn fe'th codwyd ar sgaffaldiau a'th roi wrth ei gilydd?" meddai Uarda wrth archwilio'r llew yn ofalus.

Uarda thought about how the lions got there.
"Were you airlifted by helicopter and dropped into position?" she asked.
"No," replied the lion.
"Did the sculptor come here with a hammer and chisel and carve you from a large rock?" asked Uarda
"Not quite" replied the lion.
"Were you carved close by?" quizzed Uarda smiling.
"Yes," cried the lion, "In a small workshop just below this bridge," just then Uarda interrupted the lion…
…"and piece by piece you were hauled up on a scaffold and stuck together?" cried Uarda, as she examined the lion closely.

Roedd Uarda wedi gweithio'r peth allan. Yn union fel yr oedd ei thad wedi gweithio allan beth oedd o'i le ar y car.

Mae pob llew wedi ei wneud allan o 11 darn carreg oedd yn eu gwneud yn haws i'w trin, ac mae pob un yn ffitio i'w gilydd yn berffaith. Roedd Uarda wedi datrys y pos.

Mae datrys posau ychydig yn debyg i beirianneg. Roedd Robert Stephenson angen adeiladu pont oedd yn ddigon cryf ac yn ddigon hir i gario trenau ar draws y Fenai. Roedd ganddo lawer o broblemau a phosau i'w datrys. Fe lwyddodd i wneud hynny'n ardderchog ac adeiladodd Bont Britannia sydd yn sefyll hyd heddiw.

Uarda had worked it out. Just like her dad had worked out what needed fixing in their car.

Each lion was made of 11 stones; each piece fitted together like a jigsaw puzzle and was easier to transport. Uarda had solved the puzzle.

Solving puzzles was a bit like engineering. Robert Stephenson wanted to build a bridge for trains to cross. The bridge needed to be big enough, strong enough and long enough to stretch across the Menai Strait. There were many problems and puzzles that he needed to find solutions for. When he did, he achieved something amazing and created the Britannia Bridge which still stands today.

Roedd yn amser i Uarda fynd, ond cyn mynd fe redodd at lew Pedwar a chusanu un o'i bawennau enfawr.
"Hwyl fawr Pedwar, fe ddof yn ôl yn fuan a rhoi enwau i chi gyd," gwaeddodd fel yr oedd yn rhedeg yn ôl at ei thad a oedd yn aros amdani wrth y car.
Aethant i mewn i'r car a gyrru dros Bont Britannia. Fel yr oeddynt yn croesi, roedd trên y Flying Scotsman yn croesi'r Bont oddi tanynt a rhoddodd y gyrrwr chwythiad ar ei ffliwt.
Yn yr ysgol ychydig ddyddiau yn ddiweddarach, cyflwynodd Uarda ei phrosiect peirianneg. Fe'i galwodd o yn,"Datrys pos y llewod", roedd yn gobeithio mynd yn ôl rhyw ddiwrnod i ddarganfod mwy am lewod un, dau a thri. Wedi'r cyfan yr oeddynt i gyd angen enw.

It was time for Uarda to go, but before she went, she ran up to lion four and kissed one of its giant paws.
"Goodbye Four, I will come back soon and give you all names," she cried as she ran back to her father who was waiting for her by the car.
They got into the car and drove across the Britannia Bridge. As they crossed, the Flying Scotsman train also crossed, and the driver gave a toot as it passed below.
A few days later at school, Uarda handed in her engineering project. She called it, "Solving the lions' puzzle". She was hoping to go back one day and find out more about lions one, two and three. After all, they all needed names.

Grym

Yn yr ysgol fe ddysgodd Uarda fod Grym yn digwydd o ganlyniad i ddau wrthrych yn dod i gysylltiad â'u gilydd. Y canlyniad yw fod effaith Tynnu neu Gwthio yn digwydd sydd yn gorfodi un neu'r ddau wrthrych i symud i rhyw gyfeiriad neu aros yn llonydd.

Fe ddysgodd hefyd am y tri Peiriant Syml a ddefnyddiwyd gan beirianwyr trwy gydol yr oesoedd i adeiladu pyramidiau a phontydd ac yn y blaen. Mae'r peiriannau syml hyn yn cynyddu'r grym trwy luosi'r ymdrech roddir i mewn ac felly yn cynyddu'r effaith a galluogi codi mwy o bwysau. Y tri peiriant yw'r cŷn hollti (wedge), y trosol a'r pwli.

Helpwch Uarad i gwblhau ei phrosiect peirianneg "Datrys Pos y Llewod"
Canfu Uarda fod pob un o'r pedwar llew wedi ei wneud allan o 11 o flociau calchfaen o Chwarel Penmon a bod un llew cyfan yn pwyso 30 tunnell – mae hynny'n gyfartal i 150 o lewod go iawn.
Symudwyd y llewod i'w lle mewn tri chymal.
Allwch chi helpu Uarda i benderfynu pa rym ddefnyddiwyd a pha beiriant syml oedd yn gwneud y gwaith?

1. Curwyd cynion hollti i mewn i dwll neu hollt yn y graig efo gordd er mwyn ei hollti'n ddarnau llai.
Beth oedd y Grym, Gwthio ynteu Tynnu?
2. Defnyddwyd trosolion i symud y blociau ar gyfer eu cario i safle'r Bont
Beth oedd y Grym, Gwthio ynteu Tynnu?
3. Defnyddiwyd pwliau i godi'r blociau i mewn ac allan o long ac i'w codi at fynedfa'r Bont.
  Beth oedd y Grym, Gwthio ynteu Tynnu?

Atebion

1. Gwthio – yn achos y cŷn hollti mae'r ordd yn gwthio'r cŷn i mewn i'r graig ac oherwydd ei siap mae'n gwthio yn erbyn y ddwy ochor i'r graig ac yn ei hollti.

2. Tynnu – yn achos y trosol, wrth dynnu ar y pen hir i far sydd a'j ben byr yn erbyn y bloc mae'r ymdrech yn cael ei luosi i roi mwy o rym.

3. Tynnu – yn achos system pwli mae'r ymdrech yn mynd i dynnu un pen i'r rhaff sydd wedyn yn cael ei luosi'n mhob darn o'r rhaff fel maent yn mynd o gwmpas olwynion y pwliau.

Force

In school Uarda learnt that a Force results when two objects come into contact with each other. The result is a Push or Pull action which causes either one or both the objects to move in a certain direction or to stop.

She also learnt about the three Simple Machines used by engineers throughout history to build everything from pyramids to bridges. These simple mechanical devices increase the force by multiplying the effort applied, thus extending the impact or increasing the lifting capacity. The three simple machines are the wedge, the lever and the pulley.

Help Uarda to do her engineering project "Solving the Lions Puzzle".

Uarda discovered that each of the four lions had been made from 11 blocks of local limestone brought down from the Penmon Quarry and that one finished stone lion weighed 30 tonnes - that's about the same as 150 live male lions all standing together!

The lions were moved in to position in three stages.

Can you help Uarda decide which force was used with which Simple Machine?

1. Wedges were hammered into slits or holes in large quarry rocks to split them into smaller stone blocks.
Was the Force used Push or Pull?

2. Levers were used to move the blocks to where they could be transported by ship.
Was the Force used Push or Pull?

3. Pulleys were used to load and unload the blocks onto the ship and to lift the carved stone blocks up to their position at the entrance of the rail bridge.
Was the Force used Push or Pull?

Answers:

1. Push - with the wedge, the hammer pushes the wedge into the rock and because of its shape, the wedge pushes sideways against each face of the rock, forcing it to split.

2. Pull – in the case of a lever, by applying the effort to the long end of a bar that has its short end against the stone block, the effort is multiplied to give a much bigger force.

3. Pull - in a pulley system, the effort is applied to one end of the rope and the effort is multiplied within each section of the rope as it goes round the various pulley wheels.

Welcome

THE PROBLEM with lists is that you can never keep everyone happy. Even we weren't happy with some of the players we had to leave out of our Football's Finest listing!

We tried to include players who have made a big impression on world football over the past four decades or so. You will no doubt have your own heroes who don't feature in our list. We could apologise for omitting some of these players, but we won't! Those dropped to the subs bench for this book may well get a run out another time!

Every single one of the guys on the following pages have certainly made a mark on my life and the game of football. I've been lucky enough to see many of them live.

Some I've hated because of their performances against England or my club team! Others I have watched in awe and admiration as they have defended, created or attacked with skills many of us mere mortals can only dream about.

All of these players have one thing in common though - they are true stars of the planet's greatest game who have carved out their own places in history!

Colin Mitchell, Editor

£6.99

WELSH WIZARD

Ryan Joseph Giggs

Birthdate: November 29, 1973
Birthplace: Cardiff
Position: Midfielder
Clubs: Manchester United
International: Wales (64 caps, 12 goals)
Did you know? In May 2008 Ryan passed the 758 game mark for Man United making him the club's record appearance holder of all time.

RYAN GIGGS is the best role model any would-be football player could ever have.

He's stayed with Manchester United since he joined them as a junior player in 1987. Ryan signed on as a professional on his 17th birthday.

But his sheer dedication to staying fit and giving his all for the Old Trafford side has earned him massive respect throughout the game.

Blessed with fantastic skills, Giggsy has been a pain in the backside of many top-flight defenders for years. He even called an end to his international career in 2007 so that he could prolong his club football.

Awarded an OBE for his services to football in 2007, he also reached a record TEN Premier League titles at the end of season 2007-08.

Giggsy is expected to move into coaching at United when he finally hangs up his boots.

He was the first player to win consecutive PFA Young Player of the Year awards (1992 and 1993) and also has four FA Cup winner's medals, two League Cup victories, two Champions League wins, seven Community Shield medals and a whole host of other silverware.

WHAT THEY SAID...

Sir Alex Ferguson, Man United manager:
"Ryan is an exceptional person who has always prepared and behaved in the right way to be a top footballer. He is phenomenal. It is not easy in the modern game for players to show such loyalty to one club."

Super Strikers

MICHAEL OWEN

Michael James Owen

Birthdate: December 14, 1979
Birthplace: Chester
Position: Striker
Clubs: Liverpool, Real Madrid, Newcastle United
International: England (current)
Did you know? Michael's Dad Terry played for Everton and Chester City and tries to get to as many games as possible to see his son play.

ENGLAND'S FOURTH-HIGHEST goalscorer of all time with 40 goals from his first 89 games, Michael Owen has proved that whoever he plays for he can find the back of the net.

The critics reckon a whole string of injuries have robbed him of the pace that saw him fly past defenders when he was younger – but Michael has shown that he is still fast enough and certainly clever enough to keep on scoring.

A natural finisher who knows how to time his runs and get into the right areas to outfox the fastest and toughest of challenges.

GARY LINEKER

Gary Winston Lineker

Birthdate: November 30, 1960
Birthplace: Leicester
Position: Striker
Clubs: Leicester City, Everton, Barcelona, Spurs, Grampus 8
International: England (80 caps, 48 goals)
Did you know? Gary ended his playing days in Japan at Grampus 8, a side then managed by Arsene Wenger.

NOW BETTER KNOWN as a Match of the Day presenter and crisp muncher, Gary was an outstanding striker who ended his career just one international goal behind Bobby Charlton, making him England's second-highest scorer ever.

A top-class poacher, he often jokes that he never scored many goals from outside of the penalty area. But five England hat-tricks during an international career that lasted from 1984 to 1992 marked him down as a deadly finisher.

England's Footballer of the Year in 1986, he won the Spanish Cup and the European Cup Winner's Cup during his time at Barcelona.

IAN RUSH

LIVERPOOL PAID a then-record £300,000 for a teenager when they signed Rushie, 18, from Chester City in 1980.

He won five league titles and three FA Cups with the Reds and scored 229 League goals for the Anfield side. He is their record goalscorer with a staggering 346 goals in all competitions.

Awarded an MBE for services to sport, he was PFA Young Player of the Year in 1983. The following year he was PFA and Football Writers Player of the Year and also won the European Golden Boot for 32 League goals.

Ian James Rush

Birthdate: October 20, 1961
Birthplace: St. Asaph, Wales
Position: Striker
Clubs: Chester, Liverpool (twice), Juventus, Leeds, Newcastle United, Sheffield United (loan), Wrexham
International: Wales (78 caps, 28 goals)
Did you know? Rushie didn't really like being in Italy and returned to Liverpool after just one season at Juventus and allegedly said: "It's like living in a foreign country." He later denied this quote.

GEOFF HURST

THE WEST HAM frontman will forever be remembered for his World Cup Final hat-trick at Wembley in 1966 that saw England lift the trophy for the first and only time.

Incredibly, he had gone into that match after only a handful of international games and wasn't regarded as the first-choice striker. He scored his hat-trick against the Germans with his head, left foot and right foot, although one of the goals was heavily disputed as to whether the ball had crossed the line.

His previous two appearances at Wembley had resulted in him winning the FA Cup and the European Cup Winner's Cup with the Hammers.

Geoffrey Charles Hurst

Birthdate: December 8, 1941
Birthplace: Ashton Under Lyne, Lancashire
Position: Striker
Clubs: West Ham, Stoke City, West Brom, Seattle Sounders
International: England (49 caps, 24 goals)
Did you know? Sir Geoff turned out for Essex against Lancashire making him the only World Cup winner to also play first-class cricket!

BRITISH LIONS

TERRY BUTCHER

Terence Ian Butcher

Birthdate: December 28, 1958
Birthplace: Singapore
Position: Central-defender
Clubs: Ipswich, Rangers, Coventry, Sunderland
International: England (77 caps, 3 goals)
Did you know? When the ex-England skipper became Coventry player-manager at the age of 31 he was the youngest manager in the League.

THE IMAGE of Butcher with his head wrapped in a blood-stained bandage and blood splattered down his shirt is etched on the memories of many supporters of all ages.

That picture probably said more than many words could about the never-say-die attitude of the centre-half noted for his heading ability and uncompromising tackles.

The blood came from a forehead injury which, although stitched, opened up during a World Cup qualifier against Sweden for Italia 90.

Butcher won the European Cup whilst playing at Ipswich Town under Bobby Robson who would later become his England manager.

JOHN TERRY

John George Terry

Birthdate: December 7, 1980
Birthplace: Barking, East London
Position: Central-defender
Clubs: Chelsea, Nottingham Forest (loan)
International: England (current)
Did you know? JT's brother Paul has played for Yeovil and Orient.

THE CHELSEA and England skipper could easily be a latter day version of Terry Butcher thanks to his sheer determination, commitment and ability to play through the pain barrier!

He's known as Mr Chelsea to the club's fans and when the Blues are up against it they know that their hard-tackling centre-half will lead from the back.

Not frightened to get in hard where it hurts, he'll also push forwards when he can, use the ball intelligently and, if there is half a chance, will be in the opposition penalty box for set-pieces.

STEVEN GERRARD

RED UNTIL HE'S DEAD! It's difficult to imagine Stevie G playing for any club other than Liverpool. He's Anfield through and through, the King of the Kop, the goalscoring, hard-tackling midfielder who now appears to be able to play anywhere. Fantastic long, defence-splitting passes and lethal rasping shots on goal are his trademarks. When his name is missing from the team sheet it means he is injured or suspended. A Reds side without him is certainly a lot weaker.

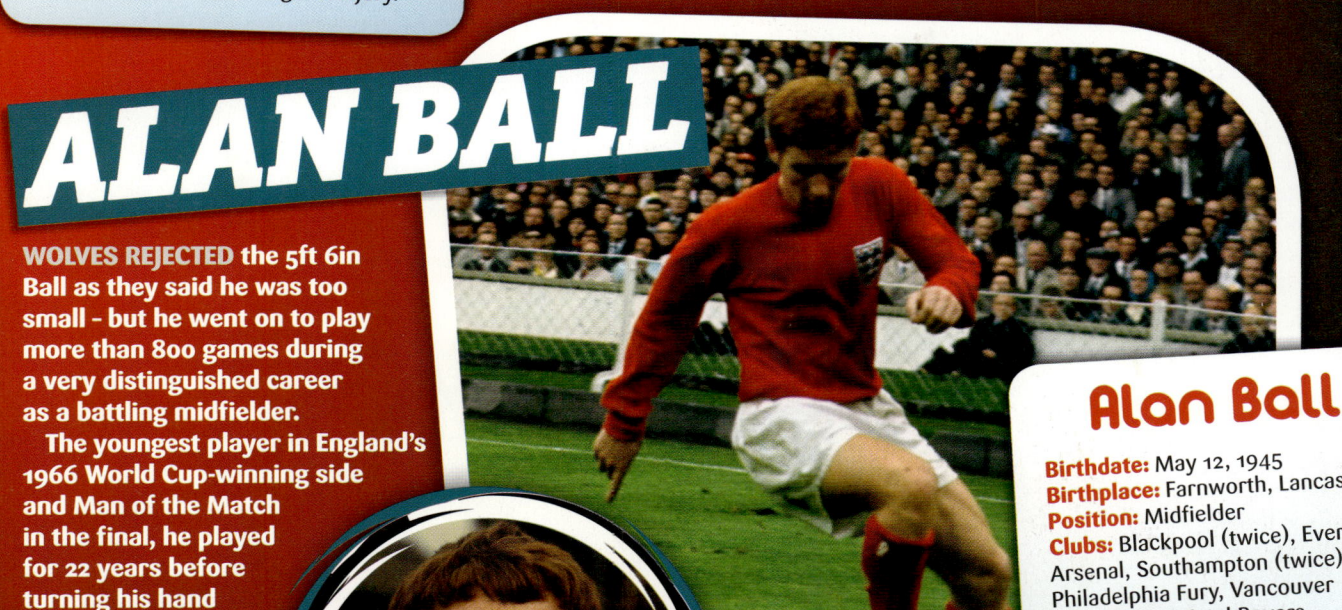

Steven George Gerrard

Birthdate: May 30, 1980
Birthplace: Whiston, Liverpool
Position: Midfielder
Clubs: Liverpool
International: England (current)
Did you know? Gerrard played and scored his first international goal in England's famous 5-1 victory in Germany during a World Cup 2002 qualifier but missed out on the finals due to a groin injury.

ALAN BALL

WOLVES REJECTED the 5ft 6in Ball as they said he was too small – but he went on to play more than 800 games during a very distinguished career as a battling midfielder.

The youngest player in England's 1966 World Cup-winning side and Man of the Match in the final, he played for 22 years before turning his hand to management.

Had successful times as boss at rivals Portsmouth and Southampton but didn't enjoy such a happy time at cash-strapped Manchester City.

Alan Ball

Birthdate: May 12, 1945
Birthplace: Farnworth, Lancashire
Position: Midfielder
Clubs: Blackpool (twice), Everton, Arsenal, Southampton (twice), Philadelphia Fury, Vancouver Whitecaps, Bristol Rovers
International: England (72 caps, 8 goals)
Did you know? When he passed away following a heart attack in April 2007, Bally became only the second member of the 1966 World Cup side to die, following Bobby Moore's death in 1993.

CLASS ACT

Robert Frederick Chelsea Moore

Birthdate: April 12, 1941
Birthplace: Barking, East London
Position: Central-defender
Clubs: West Ham, Fulham, San Antonio Thunder, Seattle Sounders
International: England (108 caps, 2 goals)
Did you know? When he died at the young age of 51 in 1993, Bobby Moore was the first member of England's 1966 World Cup-winning squad to pass away.

CAPTAIN OF CLUB and country, West Ham's most famous son earned his place in history as the man who led England to victory in the 1966 World Cup Final at Wembley.

Although the win against Germany was his finest moment, the cultured defender was highly rated for his reading of the game rather than his natural ability.

Forget speed, aggression or tough tackling. Moore made playing the game look like a walk in the park. Appointed England skipper in 1964 at the age of 22 and in only his 12th game, he would also win the Football Writers Player of the Year award.

In 1966 he became the first footballer to win the BBC TV Sports Personality of the Year award and it would be 1990 before another football player – Paul Gascoigne – lifted the famous trophy.

Moore also skippered England to the quarter-finals of the World Cup in 1970 and by 1973, 11 years after his international debut, he had notched 100 caps.

His 108th appearance in November 1973 made him England's most-capped player at the time. He skippered the team a record 90 times.

WHAT THEY SAID...

Sir Geoff Hurst, team-mate for club and country:
"Bobby Moore is the best player I ever played with. We've not produced another English-born central-defender who has come close to him. He never got uptight or under pressure, not even in the big games. In fact, in the big games you could guarantee that he would play even better."

Fab Forwards

EUSEBIO

Eusebio Da Silva Ferreira

Birthdate: January 25, 1942
Birthplace: Lourenco Marques, Mozambique
Position: Striker
Clubs: Sporting Lourenco Marques, Benfica, Rhode Island Oceaneers, Boston Minutemen, Monterrey, Beira-Mar, Toronto Metros-Croatia, Las Vegas Quicksilver
International: Portugal (64 caps, 41 goals)
Did you know? After his blistering goals performance in the 1966 World Cup – his only finals – he had a wax model created in his honour which was displayed at the famous Madame Tussauds in London.

IT WAS WAY BACK in 1961 that Eusebio was spotted playing in Mozambique and was bought by Portuguese side Benfica for just £7,500. In today's money he would have been worth world record fees.

Speed, skill and power meant he was virtually unstoppable once he got even a glimpse of goal – 319 goals in 313 games for Benfica tell their own story!

Even more goals followed in the 1966 World Cup, Portugal's first appearance in the finals, where Euesbio was the top scorer with nine goals, including two against reigning champions Brazil and four against North Korea!

LUIS FIGO

Luis Filipe Madeira Caeiro Figo

Birthdate: November 4, 1972
Birthplace: Almada, Portugal
Position: Midfielder
Clubs: Sporting Portugal, Barcelona, Real Madrid, Inter Milan
International: Portugal (127 caps, 32 goals)
Did you know? Juventus and Parma both claimed they had signed the player in 1995 and that led to Figo being banned from transferring to Italy for two years.

THE 2000 EUROPEAN Player of the Year and 2001 World Player of the Year, Figo produces his best performances on the right wing.

Many defenders have been left stunned with his tricky play and dribbling skills as Figo has left them stranded.

During his time at Barcelona he skippered the side and won the UEFA Cup Winner's Cup and two La Liga titles. But then he stunned Barca fans with a then world record £38m move to big rivals Real Madrid. Two more titles and the European Cup were among the silverware he won at the Bernabeau.

He left Madrid in 2005 to join Inter Milan for £6m and has collected three league titles, the Italian Cup and three Italian Supercups.

RAUL

REAL MADRID'S youngest-ever player when he made his debut at 17 years and four months, Raul is a rare one-club man.

He is the Spanish league's highest-ever scorer with in excess of 200 goals, helped by the fact that up to the middle of the 2008-09 season he has never received a red card.

He has scored in the World Cup finals of 1998, 2002 and 2006 and has captained Spain for whom he is the record goalscorer.

Raul, who can play as a winger or striker, quit the international scene after the 2006 World Cup finals.

Raul Gonzalez Blanco

Birthdate: June 27, 1977
Birthplace: Madrid
Position: Forward
Clubs: Real Madrid
International: Spain (102 caps, 44 goals)
Did you know? Besides being a three times winner of the European Cup, he was the first player to score 50 goals in the tournament and is the event's leading scorer (63 and counting).

PAVEL NEDVED

A PLAY-MAKING, attacking midfielder, Nedved was European Footballer of the Year in 2003.

His all-action performances and his distinctive flowing hair made him a player who stood out from the crowd. Nedved was a beaten finalist in Euro 96 and semi-finalist in 2004.

Although he had retired from international competition, the player did a U-turn to help the Czechs qualify for the 2006 World Cup finals. He quit again after the finals and refused to turn out for Euro 2008.

Pavel Nedved

Birthdate: August 30, 1972
Birthplace: Cheb, Czech Republic
Position: Midfielder
Clubs: Sparta Prague, Lazio, Juventus
International: Czech Republic (91 caps, 18 goals)
Did you know? Nedved has won one Italian title with Lazio and four with Juventus – although he lost two of the latter ones over the match-fixing scandal.

BRILLIANT BRAZILIANS

Ricardo Izecson dos Santos Leite

Birthdate: April 22, 1982
Birthplace: Brasilia
Position: Midfielder
Clubs: Sao Paulo, AC Milan
International: Brazil (current)
Did you know? Kaka is a devout Christian and even his goal celebration involves him pointing to the sky to acknowledge God.

KAKA

KAKA MADE HIS Brazil debut at the age of 19 and now has more than 60 caps to his name.

With in excess of 300 club appearances already under his belt he's proved to be a shrewd signing by AC Milan who bought him for about £5m in 2003.

At the time the club's owner said the fee was "peanuts" - which has proved to be the case for a player who is now worth at least six times his original fee.

Kaka won the Ballon d'Or and FIFA World Player of the Year awards in 2007 and can count the 2007 Champions League, Italian Super Cup and 2002 World cup among his awards.

ZICO

LONG BEFORE the days of "Bend it like Beckham", Zico was dribbling past the opposition as if they weren't there and curling free-kicks passed keepers with incredible accuracy.

Just take a look at his incredible international scoring record which shows a goal in less than every one and a half games - and he wasn't even an out-and-out striker!

Represented Brazil at the 1978, 1982 and 1986 World Cups, tournaments that the planet's greatest team never won. He got some compensation in the form of the World Player of the Year award in 1983.

Arthur Antunes Coimbra

Birthdate: March 3, 1953
Birthplace: Rio de Janeiro
Position: Midfielder
Clubs: Flamengo (twice), Udinese, Sumitomo Metals, Kashima Antlers
International: Brazil (88 caps, 66 goals)
Did you know? Zico played 1,180 games between 1971 and 1994.

RONALDINHO

ONLY A HANDFUL of players can make you sit on the edge of your seat in anticipation of what they might do next. Ronnie is one of them!

His mesmerising ball skills, jinking runs, cheeky passes and wicked attempts on goal make him an attacking midfielder who can change games with just a few seconds of blistering skill.

He turned down Manchester United in 2003 to join Barcelona and went on to become World Player of the Year in 2004 and 2005. He also collected two La Liga titles and was a Champions League winner in 2006.

Ronaldo de Assis Moreira

Birthdate: March 21, 1980
Birthplace: Porto Alegre
Position: Midfielder
Clubs: Gremio, Paris Saint German, Barcelona, AC Milan
International: Brazil (current)
Did you know? Ronaldinho almost ended up on loan at St. Mirren in the Scottish Premier League but that plan was scuppered by a row over false passports!

SOCRATES

NAMED BY WORLD SOCCER magazine as one of the 100 best footballers ever, Socrates was a two-footed midfield general.

A bit like Steven Gerrard in today's game, he ran the midfield, laid on goals and scored his fair share too.

Captained Brazil at the 1982 and 1986 World Cup finals and proved he was no slouch off the pitch either as he studied to become a doctor, a career he now follows back in his home country.

Sócrates Brasileiro Sampaio da Souza Vieira de Oliveira

Birthdate: February 19, 1954
Birthplace: Ribeirao Preto
Position: Midfielder
Clubs: Botafogo, Corinthians, Fiorentina, Flamengo, Santos
International: Brazil (63 caps, 25 goals)
Did you know? More than ten years after hanging up his boots, Socrates turned out for Garforth Town in the Northern Counties East Football League. He played just 12 minutes against Tadcaster Albion in 2004.

MARADONA

MAGIC MARADONA

Diego Armando Maradona

Birthdate: October 30, 1960
Birthplace: Buenos Aires
Position: Striker
Clubs: Boca Juniors (twice), Barcelona, Napoli, Sevilla, Newell's Old Boys
International: Argentina (91 caps, 34 goals)
Did you know? Maradona presented a regular and successful two-hour chat show on Argentine TV, "The Night of the Number Ten", which was named after his No.10 shirt.

THE 1986 WORLD CUP FINALS will forever by remembered by many fans as Maradona's magic moment – although England supporters believe he got away with murder!

He scored five goals as he captained Argentina to victory – two of them against the Three Lions in the quarter-finals.

The first was his infamous "Hand of God" goal where he admitted pushing the ball into the net with his hand. There was no disputing his second as he ran from his own half and past seven England players!

Maradona is only 5ft 5in tall but despite his height was a deadly attacking midfielder or striker. He was joint FIFA Player of the Century alongside Pele.

He was Argentina's youngest international when he turned out at the age of 16.

Two South America Player of the Year awards followed before a move to Barcelona for a then-record £5m fee. He won La Liga, the league cup and Spanish Supercup at Barca.

Another world record £6.9m fee took him to Napoli where he won an Italian league and cup double, followed by the UEFA Cup and other honours.

He set a then-record of playing in 21 consecutive World Cup finals games but his career came to an end after the second of two drug scandals.

WHAT THEY SAID...

Paolo Maldini, Italy and AC Milan's No.1 defender: "The best I ever played against was Maradona. He is the striker who put me in most difficulty on the pitch."

17

The Four Rs

WAYNE ROONEY

Wayne Mark Rooney

Birthdate: October 24, 1985
Birthplace: Liverpool
Position: Striker
Clubs: Everton, Man United
International: England (current)
Did you know? The Roonster scored a Champions League hat-trick against Fenerbahce on his Manchester United debut in September 2004.

IT'S HARD TO BELIEVE Wayne is still just 23-years-old with plenty of years still ahead of him.

An established England player, he's also proved he is more than just a frontman having adapted to playing wide or behind one man upfront.

Wayne's got bags of skill, good vision and has managed to curb his ruthless streak which saw him see red a few times earlier in his career. But he hasn't lost the edge that determination gave him.

He cost around £30m when Man United bought him from Everton. Under Sir Alex Ferguson his skills have been polished, but could get brighter!

CRISTIANO RONALDO

Cristiano Ronaldo Dos Santos Aveiro

Birthdate: February 5, 1985
Birthplace: Madeira
Position: Winger
Clubs: Sporting, Man United
International: Portugal (current)
Did you know? Man United players allegedly begged Fergie to sign Ronaldo after playing against him in a friendly. What they didn't realise is that their boss had already scouted the player.

LOVE HIM OR hate him you certainly can't deny the Portugal midfielder has awesome skills and lethal finishing.

Ronnie plays best when he's wide right, serving up defence-splitting crosses for his team-mates or dancing his way past the opposition to reach scoring positions.

He's often been criticised for going to ground a bit too easily under strong challenges but at the speed he travels one good knock and he's sent sprawling.

There's fewer step-overs and showboating nowadays, probably down to Fergie dishing out advice. He's got enough dribbling skills and ability at free-kicks to keep most supporters happy!

ROBINHO

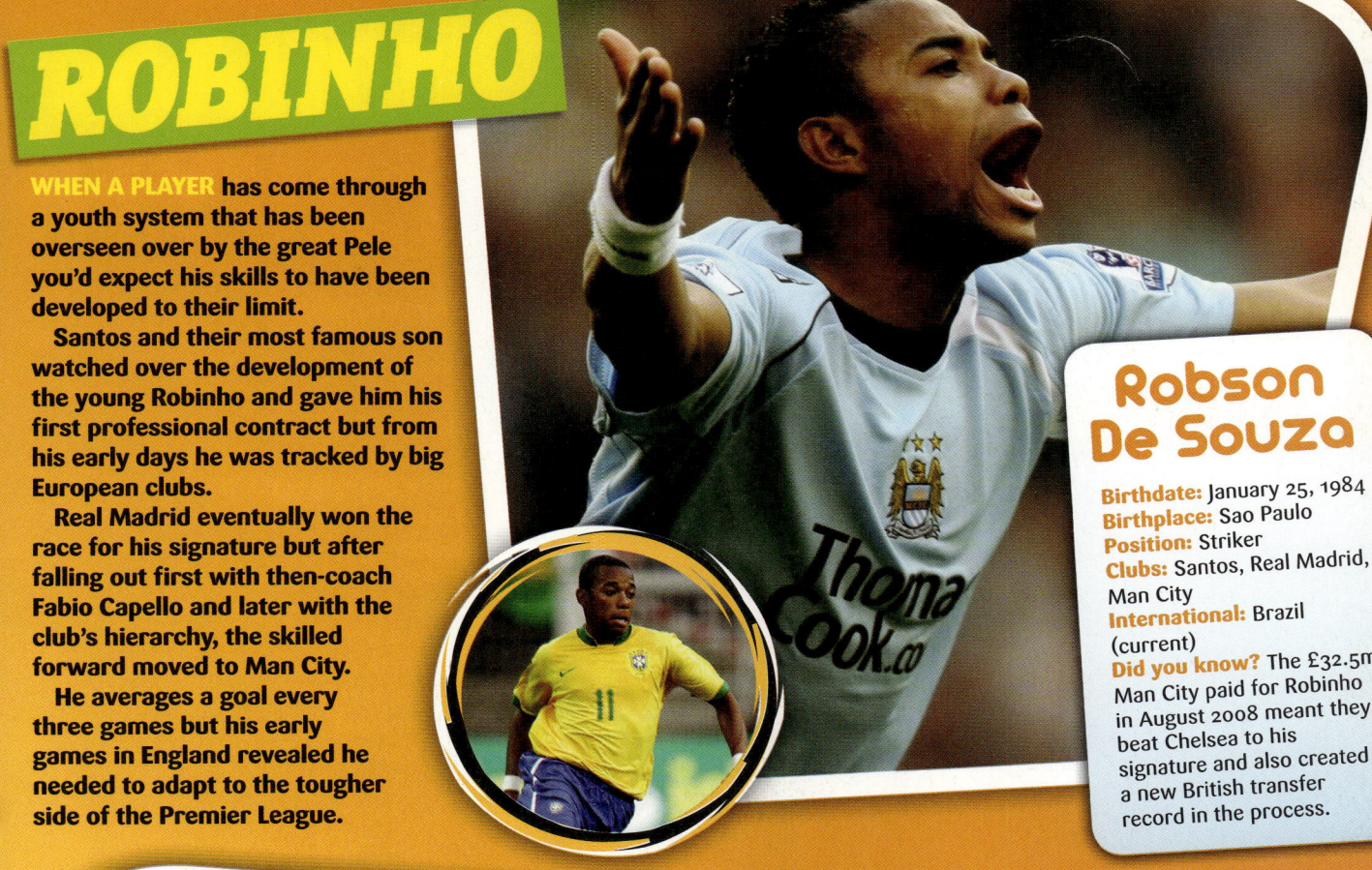

WHEN A PLAYER has come through a youth system that has been overseen over by the great Pele you'd expect his skills to have been developed to their limit.

Santos and their most famous son watched over the development of the young Robinho and gave him his first professional contract but from his early days he was tracked by big European clubs.

Real Madrid eventually won the race for his signature but after falling out first with then-coach Fabio Capello and later with the club's hierarchy, the skilled forward moved to Man City.

He averages a goal every three games but his early games in England revealed he needed to adapt to the tougher side of the Premier League.

Robson De Souza

Birthdate: January 25, 1984
Birthplace: Sao Paulo
Position: Striker
Clubs: Santos, Real Madrid, Man City
International: Brazil (current)
Did you know? The £32.5m Man City paid for Robinho in August 2008 meant they beat Chelsea to his signature and also created a new British transfer record in the process.

RONALDO

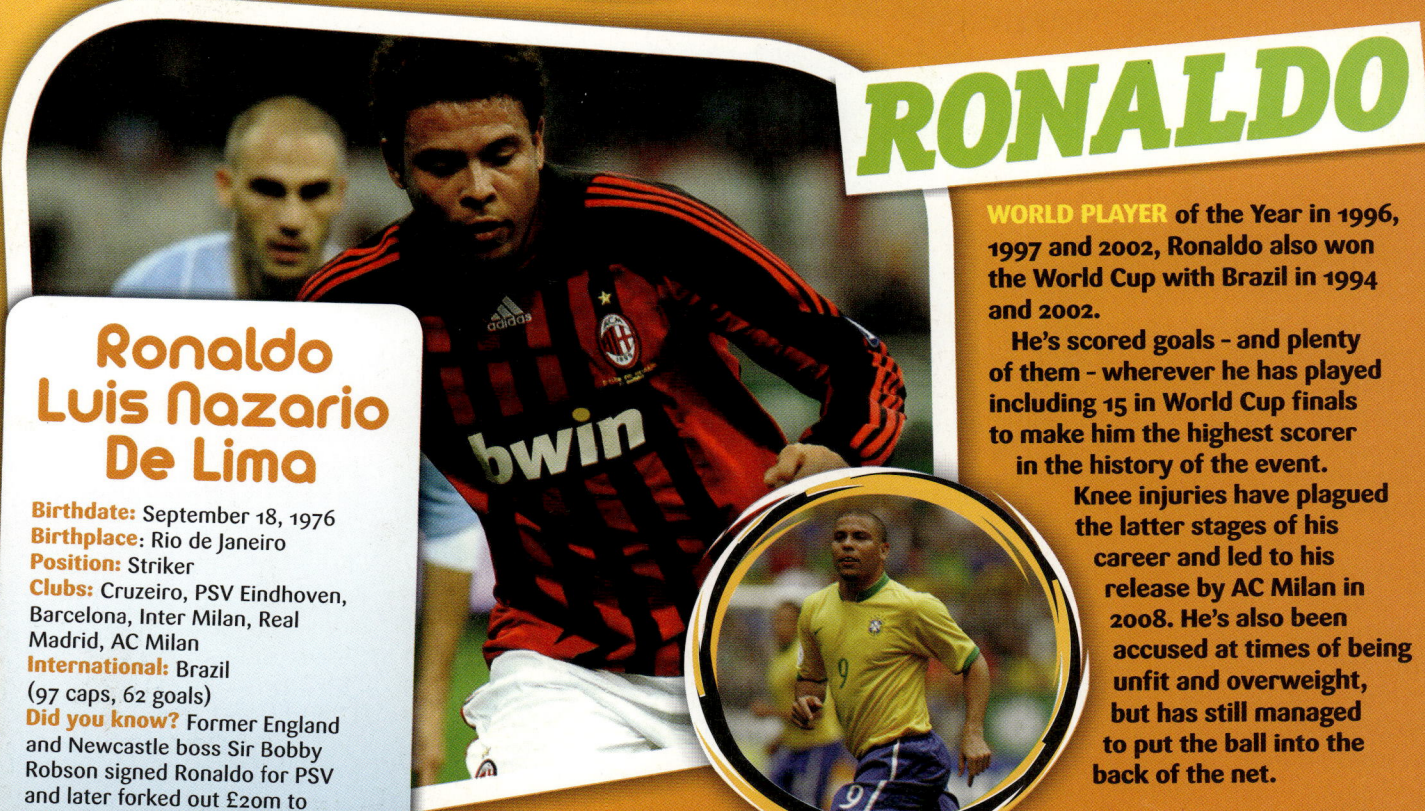

WORLD PLAYER of the Year in 1996, 1997 and 2002, Ronaldo also won the World Cup with Brazil in 1994 and 2002.

He's scored goals - and plenty of them - wherever he has played including 15 in World Cup finals to make him the highest scorer in the history of the event.

Knee injuries have plagued the latter stages of his career and led to his release by AC Milan in 2008. He's also been accused at times of being unfit and overweight, but has still managed to put the ball into the back of the net.

Ronaldo Luis Nazario De Lima

Birthdate: September 18, 1976
Birthplace: Rio de Janeiro
Position: Striker
Clubs: Cruzeiro, PSV Eindhoven, Barcelona, Inter Milan, Real Madrid, AC Milan
International: Brazil (97 caps, 62 goals)
Did you know? Former England and Newcastle boss Sir Bobby Robson signed Ronaldo for PSV and later forked out £20m to take him to Barcelona.

DUTCH MASTERS

JOHAN CRUYFF

THE LEGENDARY No.14 had bags of skill and pace but it was his ability to drive on his team-mates at both club and international level that made him an outstanding player.

His determination helped Ajax to eight Dutch league titles, five domestic cups, three European Cups, two UEFA Super Cups. He also won La Liga with Barcelona along with the Copa del Ray, plus a league and cup double on his return to Holland with PSV.

Three times European Footballer of the Year he was a member of the Holland side beaten in the 1974 World Cup Final. Retired after 752 club appearances and 425 goals.

Later became the most successful manager in Barcelona's history.

Hendrik Johannes Cruijff
Birthdate: April 25, 1947
Birthplace: Amsterdam
Position: Midfielder
Clubs: Ajax (twice), Barcelona, Los Angeles Aztecs, Washington Diplomats, Levante, Feyenoord
International: Holland (48 caps, 33 goals)
Did you know? Cruijff is the Dutch spelling of his name. His son Jordi played for Man United and Barcelona before going into the Cruyff fashion business.

MARCO VAN BASTEN

THREE TIMES European Footballer of the Year and the 1992 World Player of the Year, van Basten was one of the finest strikers of all time.

After 277 goals in 370 club games his career was ended by an ankle injury at the age of 30 in 1995. His spectacular goals will never be forgotten.

His finishing helped Ajax to the UEFA Cup Winners Cup, three Dutch titles and three Dutch cups. He was twice a European Cup winner with AC Milan, along with three Serie A titles, three Italian Super Cups, two European Supercups and two Intercontinental Cup wins.

Marcel Van Basten
Birthdate: October 31, 1964
Birthplace: Utrecht
Position: Striker
Clubs: Ajax, AC Milan
International: Holland (58 caps, 24 goals)
Did you know? Van Basten coached Holland for four years before becoming boss at Ajax.

Johannes Jacobus Neeskens

Birthdate: September 15, 1951
Birthplace: Heemstede
Position: Midfielder
Clubs: RCH, Ajax, Barcelona, New York Cosmos, Groningen, Minnesota Strikers, Fort Lauderdale Sun, FC Baar, FC Zug
International: Holland (47 caps, 17 goals)
Did you know? Neeskens actually played at right-back for Ajax in the European Cup victory over Panathinaikos in 1971.

JOHAN NEESKENS

A MIDFIELD partner for Cruyff at both Ajax and Barcelona, the pair also played together for Holland. The hard-working Neeskens allowed his partner to get forward more, although he was no slouch in the skill stakes.

He played in Holland's impressive 1974 and 1978 World Cup finals sides and was a member of the Ajax team that won three European Cups. Also earned a Spanish Cup medal and European Cup Winners Cup victory during his time at Barca. Like Cruyff he moved into management and coaching, including roles with both Barcelona and Holland.

RUUD GULLIT

MOST FANS remember the dreadlocked Gullitt as a raiding midfielder. But the skilled all-rounder played virtually every position expect keeper!

Despite his 6ft 3in frame he had great balance, speed and skill. His strength meant he was exceptionally difficult to knock off the ball.

Skipper of his country's Euro 1988 winning side, he won four Dutch titles, a Dutch Cup, three Serie A, three Italian Supercups, two Champions Leagues, a European Supercup, Italian Cup and the 1997 FA Cup during his time with Chelsea who he would later manage.

Twice World Player of the Year and twice Dutch Player of the Year he hit 235 goals in 611 career games.

Ruud Dil Gullit

Birthdate: September 1, 1962
Birthplace: Amsterdam
Position: Midfielder
Clubs: Haarlem, Feyenoord, PSV Eindhoven, AC Milan (twice), Sampdoria (twice), Chelsea
International: Holland (66 caps, 17 goals)
Did you know? When he guided Chelsea to the FA Cup in 1997 as their player-manager, it was the club's first major trophy in 26 years. He also helped them to sixth and then runners-up in the Premiership before being sacked.

KILLER KEANE

YOU DON'T MESS with Roy Keane! As a player and as a manager Keano has proved that he has skill, aggression, determination and is a man of principles.

Long-serving captain of Man United and Republic of Ireland, the midfielder scrapper with an eye for an often spectacular and important goal, knew he was either loved or hated. But he didn't care!

Keano had a job to do and he did it well. He demands respect but he also gives respect to those who do their jobs and do them well.

As a player he was totally committed to the cause. Nothing would make him change course once he had an aim, something he proved with seven Premier League titles and four FA Cups during his 12 years at Old Trafford.

He's fallen out with his own team-mates and had highly publicised clashes with Sir Alex Ferguson, former England skipper Alan Shearer and Arsenal captain Patrick Vieira.

A key player at the 1994 World Cup finals, he was sent home under a cloud after a much publicised and heated row with boss Mick McCarthy at the 2002 tournament. But this was just Keane standing up for his team-mates, saying they had not been treated as they deserved.

He's now boss of Sunderland where he turned around the club's fortunes.

Roy Maurice Keane

Birthdate: August 10, 1971
Birthplace: Cork, Republic of Ireland
Position: Midfielder
Clubs: Cobh Ramblers, Nottingham Forest, Man United, Celtic
International: Republic of Ireland (66 caps, 9 goals)
Did you know? Keano played just ten games for Celtic before hanging up his boots but it meant one of his dreams had come true – he had pulled on the white and green hoops of his boyhood heroes.

WHAT THEY SAID...

Sir Alex Ferguson, the boss who bought him for £2m: "He is very driven, a great influence and very determined. He was fantastic to me, the best player I had. I can see myself in Roy and Roy in me."

ROY KEANE

Red Devils

ERIC CANTONA

Eric Daniel Pierre Cantona

Birthdate: May 24, 1966
Birthplace: Marseille
Position: Forward
Clubs: Auxerre, Martigues (loan), Bordeaux (loan), Montpellier (loan), Nimes, Leeds, Man United
International: France (45 caps, 20 goals)
Did you know? The season Cantona missed out on a title he was suspended from the game for nine months for launching a kung-fu kick on a Crystal Palace fan who hurled verbal abuse at him.

FOUR LEAGUE TITLES in five years made Cantona "King Eric" among Manchester United fans. He arrived at Old Trafford for a bargain £1.2m from bitter rivals Leeds in 1992 and proved to be the catalyst to kick start United's trail of success which has continued to the present day. A vastly skilled player, he was never far away from controversy but his goals and assists made him a vital cog in Sir Alex Ferguson's side.

ANDY COLE

Andrew Alexander Cole

Birthdate: October 15, 1971
Birthplace: Nottingham
Position: Striker
Clubs: Arsenal, Fulham (loan), Bristol City, Newcastle, Manchester United, Blackburn, Fulham, Man City, Portsmouth, Birmingham City (loan), Sunderland, Burnley (loan), Nottingham Forest.
International: England (15 caps, 1 goal)
Did you know? Kevin Keegan almost sparked a riot by Newcastle fans when he sold Cole to Man United in a deal worth £7m - but he won back the supporters by bringing in £15m Alan Shearer.

ANDY COLE WAS a little known but promising striker at Bristol City when Newcastle bought him for a then club record £1.75m.

He scored 12 goals in 12 games for the Magpies and a total of 41 goals in all competitions as they reached the Premiership the following season, to set a new club best.

Just two years after his move to the North East, Cole was sold to Manchester United where he scored 93 goals in 195 games, forming a lethal partnership with Dwight Yorke.

BOBBY CHARLTON

ALTHOUGH A MIDFIELDER, Bobby Charlton was an accomplished goal scorer with a thunderbolt of a shot.

A member of England's 1966 World Cup-winning side he joined Man United when he was just 17 and stayed there for a further 17 years. He won three league titles, an FA Cup and a European Cup and is today still a director at Old Trafford.

European Footballer of the Year in 1966, he scored 247 goals for United in a record-breaking 758 appearances. His record was only recently broken by Ryan Giggs.

Robert Charlton

Birthdate: October 11, 1937
Birthplace: Ashington, Northumberland
Position: Midfielder
Clubs: Manchester United, Preston, Waterford United
International: England (106 caps, 49 games)
Did you know? Charlton's younger brother Jack, who played for Leeds United, was also a member of the England 1966 World Cup-winning side.

DAVID BECKHAM

David Robert Joseph Beckham

Birthdate: May 2, 1975
Birthplace: Leytonstone, East London
Position: Midfielder
Clubs: Manchester United, Preston (loan), Real Madrid, LA Galaxy, AC Milan (loan)
International: England (current)
Did you know? Having passed the 100 England cap mark in 2008 Becks will be hoping to set a new Three Lions best. Peter Shilton is the current record holder with 125 caps.

ONE OF THE WORLD'S highest paid footballers, Beckham is a global brand and probably the best-known player on the planet.

He has skippered England 58 times and has also worn the armband for Man United for whom he made 319 appearances during his decade with the club before a £25m move to Real Madrid in 2003.

Becks won La Liga with Madrid in 2006-07 before leaving to join LA Galaxy. His Madrid shirt sales reportedly paid for his time in Spain.

Some 250,000 Galaxy shirts were sold before the star even started to earn some of his reported £25m a-year salary in LA!

FRENCH CONNECTIONS

THIERRY HENRY

Thierry Daniel Henry

Birthdate: August 17, 1977
Birthplace: Essonne, France
Position: Striker
Clubs: Monaco, Juventus, Arsenal, Barcelona
International: France (current)
Did you know? Thierry has won more than 100 caps for France and has almost averaged a goal every other game.

A WINGER CONVERTED to a striker by Arsenal boss Arsene Wenger, Thierry became a record-breaking goal scorer during his time with the Gunners. Pace and skill would often see him working out wide or pulling into the centre, rifling in goals as if he'd been a natural striker all of his life.

He smashed Ian Wright's goals record for the club and set a new Arsenal best of 266 goals. He was twice PFA Players' Player of the Year and three times Football Writers' Footballer of the Year.

MICHEL PLATINI

A GOAL-SCORING midfielder who not only dictated the play but also had amazing passing and free-kick abilities, Platini was a megastar even before he hit the world stage in 1978.

His greatest moments came in the 1984 European Championships held in his home country where he scored nine goals in just five goals.

His team went on to win the tournament but for the watching world Platini was the star of the finals as France lifted their first international trophy.

Michel Francois Platini

Birthdate: June 21, 1955
Birthplace: Joeuf, France
Position: Midfielder
Clubs: Nancy, Saint Etienne, Juventus
International: France (72 caps, 41 goals)
Did you know? Platini scored 312 goals in 580 club career appearances, not a bad return for a midfielder!

ZINEDINE ZIDANE

Zinedine Yazid Zidane

Birthdate: June 23, 1972
Birthplace: Marseille
Position: Midfielder
Clubs: Cannes, Girondins Bordeaux, Juventus, Real Madrid
International: France (109 caps, 31 goals)
Did you know? ZZ's World Cup Final dismissal was the 14th of his career. He was the fourth player red-carded in a final but the first sent off in extra time.

DESPITE BEING sent-off in the final game of his career - the 2006 World Cup Final - ZZ can still be rated as one of the greatest midfielders of recent times. The creative, attacking midfielder head-butted Italian Marco Materazzi in extra-time to get his marching orders. He was still voted best player of the competition. Three times World Player of the Year, a European Footballer of the Year and winner with France of the 1998 World Cup and European Championships in 2000, he also got Champions League medal with Real Madrid in 2002.

LILIAN THURAM

THE MOST-CAPPED player in French football history, Lilian Thuram, won silverware in France, Italy and Spain.

The French West Indies-born star also struck gold with France at World Cup 1998 and Euro 2000.

Captaining his country at Euro 2008, he reached a record 16 appearances for the tournament, a best that was equalled a few days later by Edwin van der Sar.

The sheer sight of Thuram was enough to frighten most forwards as he was an intimidating figure on the pitch.

But away from football he is an unassuming man who believes in fighting for the rights of individuals.

Ruddy Lilian Thuram-Ulien

Birthdate: January 1, 1972
Birthplace: Guadeloupe
Position: Defender
Clubs: Monaco, Parma, Juventus, Barcelona
International: France (142 caps, 2 goals)
Did you know? Thuram was expected to end his career during 2008-09 with Paris Saint Germain but had to bring the curtain down early after it was discovered he has a heart problem.

ALAN SHEARER

SUPER SHEARER

Alan Shearer

Birthdate: August 13, 1970
Birthplace: Newcastle
Position: Striker
Clubs: Southampton, Blackburn, Newcastle
International: England (63 caps, 30 goals)
Did you know? A huge banner saying "Thanks for ten great years" was draped across the Gallowgate end of the ground, where there is Shearer's Bar, during the month before his testimonial game.

BIG AL HAS GONE down in history for smashing all sorts of scoring records.

He is the Premier League's highest scorer of all time with 260 goals, a total that is highly unlikely to be beaten.

Shearer is also Newcastle's record scorer with 206 goals, the last of those coming in the derby clash against Sunderland in April 2006. That was his final game as he was injured.

Newcastle missed out on signing the young Shearer as he moved more than 300 miles south to join Southampton.

He scored a hat-trick against Arsenal on his debut in 1988.

His upper body strength, his ability to hold onto the ball and his incredible eye for goal soon attracted the scout.

In 1992, Blackburn, then managed by Kenny Dalglish, and backed by the millions of Jack Walker, forked out a British record £3.3m for Shearer who rejected Man United. The striker helped Rovers to the Premiership title in 1995 before a world record transfer of £15m to home town club Newcastle.

Once again he had turned down Man United and became a legend at St. James' Park.

WHAT THEY SAID...

Former Newcastle boss Sir Bobby Robson: "He's a tough lad, a strong boy and he's obviously strong mentally. He had everything you would want from a professional. He won balls in the air, held it up well, had a lot of good movement and scored some outstanding goals."

Geordie Geniuses

BRYAN ROBSON

Bryan Robson
Birthdate: January 11, 1957
Birthplace: Chester-le-Street
Position: Midfielder
Clubs: West Brom, Man United, Middlesbrough
International: England (90 caps, 26 goals)
Did you know? During his time as manager of West Brom, the Baggies became the first Premier League side to be bottom of the league at Christmas and avoid relegation.

THE LONGEST-SERVING Man United captain and the earner of the third-highest number of caps as England skipper. It's little wonder Bryan Robson was known at Captain Marvel.

Three FA Cups, two Premier League titles and a European Cup Winner's Cup victory put Robbo into Old Trafford history. But most fans remember his crunching midfield displays that were often capped with cracking goals.

Three broken legs and a whole host of other injuries – often picked up due to his sheer determination to win – restricted his appearances for both clubs and country.

PAUL GASCOIGNE

GAZZA IS ONE of the finest midfielder players England has produced. Sadly, his potential was never fully realised due to injuries and off-field pranks.

After just three years at Newcastle he was sold to Spurs for a then British record £2.3m before moving on to Lazio for £5.5m. A move to Rangers for £4m established his credentials as a battling but skilful midfielder.

First selected for England by fellow Geordie Sir Bobby Robson, Gazza is probably best remembered for flicking the ball over Scotland defender Colin Hendry, going round the player and then scoring during Euro 96.

Paul John Gascoigne
Birthdate: May 27, 1967
Birthplace: Gateshead
Position: Midfielder
Clubs: Newcastle United, Tottenham, Lazio, Rangers, Middlesbrough, Everton, Burnley, Gansu Tianma, Boston United
International: England (57 caps, 10 goals)
Did you know? Gazza allegedly agreed to join Man United before moving to Spurs but Fergie missed out on his man when he went on holiday before the deal was done!

CHRIS WADDLE

Christopher Roland Waddle

Birthdate: December 14, 1960
Birthplace: Felling
Position: Winger
Clubs: Newcastle, Tottenham, Marseille, Sheff Wed, Falkirk, Bradford City, Sunderland, Burnley, Torquay, Worksop
International: England (62 caps, 6 goals)
Did you know? Waddler was still playing local football at the age of 40-plus!

IT WAS DURING his time sweeping up in a pie factory that Waddler was snatched from non-League Tow Law for £1,000 to play for Newcastle United.

They later sold him to Spurs for more than £500,000 before he went to Marseille for £4.5m!

The gangly winger's movements were so deceptive he appeared slow on the pitch but with a quick drop of his shoulder he left many defenders fooled as he sailed smoothly past them.

Still a legend at all of his first four clubs, it's still possible to see Waddle graffiti scrawled on walls in Marseille where he helped the French side to three league titles.

PETER BEARDSLEY

Peter Andrew Beardsley

Birthdate: January 18, 1961
Birthplace: Newcastle
Position: Forward
Clubs: Carlisle, Vancouver Whitecaps, Man United, Newcastle United (twice), Liverpool, Everton, Bolton, Man City (loan), Fulham, Hartlepool, Melbourne Knights, Doncaster.
International: England (59 caps, 9 goals)
Did you know? Manchester United seldom let a good player slip through their fingers – but Beardo is one who did escape their selection process. He joined Vancouver before returning to home town club Newcastle for just £150,000 in 1983. He would later cost them almost £2m when he returned from Everton.

MANY NEWCASTLE FANS firmly believe that Beardo is the greatest player to ever wear the famous black and white stripes during his two spells with the club.

A skilled midfielder who appeared all over the pitch during a game, showing incredible energy levels, Peter the Great was both a creator and scorer of spectacular goals.

He departed from the Geordies for Liverpool for a then British record £1.9m and won two league titles, an FA Cup winner's medal and three Charity Shields.

He is such a popular player that he was even forgiven for moving across Stanley Park to Liverpool's bitter rivals Everton!

GREAT GERMANS

FRANZ BECKENBAUER

NICKNAMED "THE KAISER" because of his style and leadership abilities, Beckenbauer captained his country more than 50 times.

Twice European Footballer of the Year, he was a World Cup-winner (1874), runner-up (1966) and in the third placed side (1970) at his three finals. He is one of only two players to achieve that collection. He would later pick up a winner's medal at the World Cup as manager of Germany in 1990. Three consecutive European Cup wins with Bayern Munich, a Cup Winner's Cup and a World Club title topped his domestic awards, plus four Bundesliga titles with Bayern and another with Hamburg. Although classed as a defender he acted more like a sweeper, or holding defensive midfielder.

Franz Anton Beckenbauer

Birthdate: September 11, 1945
Birthplace: Munich
Position: Defender
Clubs: Bayern Munich, New York Cosmos (twice), Hamburg
International: Germany (103 caps, 14 goals)
Did you know? Beckenbauer was four times German Footballer of the Year, in 1966, 1968, 1974 and 1976.

JURGEN KLINSMANN

GERMANY'S PLAYER of the Year in 1988 earned a move to Inter Milan for the following season where he was part of the Serie A-winning side.

Goals and success followed him during spells with top sides in Europe. In 1995 he was Player of the Year in England after one season with Spurs.

At White Hart Lane he was accused by opposition fans of being a diver but proved some Germans do have a sense of humour by celebrating goals with a diving celebration. He hit 21 goals during his first spell at Tottenham.

A World Cup-winner in 1990 and European Championship victor in 1996, he later managed Germany to third in the 2006 World Cup.

Jurgen Klinsmann

Birthdate: July 30, 1964
Birthplace: Goppingen
Position: Striker
Clubs: Stuttgart Kickers, Vfb Stuttgart, Inter Milan, Monaco, Tottenham (twice), Bayern Munich, Sampdoria, Orange County Blue Star
International: Germany (108 caps, 47 goals)
Did you know? During his first stint with Spurs, Klinsmann would drive around London in a clapped out VW Beetle so that he wouldn't be easily recognised by fans.

LOTHAR MATTHAUS

Lothar Herbert Matthaus

Birthdate: March 21, 1961
Birthplace: Erlangan
Position: Midfielder
Clubs: Borussia Monchengladbach,
International: Germany (150 caps, 23 goals)
Did you know? He was captain of Germany from 1987 to 1994, although he would remain in the international side for France 98 and Euro 2000.

THE BATTLING MIDFIELDER set a best when he appeared in FIVE World Cup finals - 1982, 1986, 1990, 1994 and 1998 - playing in a total of 25 games.

The European and Germany Player of the Year titles both came his way in 1990 and a year later he was the first-ever World Player of the Year. He again won the German Player title in 1999.

He could also play as a defender or sweeper and was 39 when he finally hung up his boots after Euro 2000, having set a new record for most appearances for Germany.

During an amazing career he picked up seven Bundesliga titles, three German Cups, the Serie A title, two UEFA Cups, a World Cup and a European Championships.

GERD MULLER

THERE AREN'T MANY international players who have scored more goals than they have won caps - so Gerd Muller's record makes him a bit special!

He also set a record of 66 goals in 74 European games and hit 582 goals in 669 career games.

Those goals helped his teams to win four Bundesliga titles, four German cups, three European Cups, an Intercontinental cup and a UEFA Cup Winner's Cup.

Add to that record a European Championship in 1972 and a World Cup victory in 1974 plus being Germany's top scorer for SEVEN seasons between 1967 and 1978, and you realise just how prolific a hitman he was!

Gerhard Muller

Birthdate: November 3, 1945
Birthplace: Nordingen
Position: Striker
Clubs: TSV Nordingen, Bayern Munich, Fort Lauderdale Strikers
International: Germany (62 caps, 68 goals)
Did you know? Muller was German Footballer of the Year in 1967 and 1969, European Footballer of the Year in 1970 and in 2000 was named at the greatest goalscorer of all time.

THE KING OF FOOTBALL

PELE'S AMAZING RECORD of 1,280 goals in 1,363 games takes some believing – but world football officials have rubber stamped this as an all-time record.

He managed so many games as he also played for club and country on international tours and even clocked up some official matches during his time in the Brazilian army.

Whatever you think about this record, the goals tally is amazing and one look at his total for Brazil will also tell you what an outstanding player this guy was!

Even with 589 goals in his 605 league and cup games for Santos before his move to America is stunning. A further 64 goals in 107 games for New York Cosmos is further proof of his uncanny ability.

Yet Pele, still the most respected footballer in the world, wasn't even regarded as an out-and-out striker. He was used as an attacking midfielder or second striker.

But he had the lot – dribbling, passing, speed, shooting ability and was a great header despite being only 5ft 8in tall.

Edison Arantes Do Nascimento

Birthdate: October 23, 1940
Birthplace: Tres Coraoes, Brazil
Position: Forward
Clubs: Santos, New York Cosmos
International: Brazil (92 caps, 77 goals)
Did you know? Big clubs tracked Pele's progress but were unable to lure him away from Brazil as the government said he was a national treasure and could not be sold!

WHAT THEY SAID...

Glen Johnson, Portsmouth and England defender: "He'd stopped playing before I was even born but I still think he's the greatest ever. As a boy I used to watch VHS tapes – there were no DVDs then – of him playing and just held him in awe."

PELE

Great Danes

PETER SCHMEICHEL

ONE OF THE GREATEST keepers ever in the history of football and arguably one of the best signings ever made for Man United by Sir Alex Ferguson.

During his eight years at Old Trafford, the Denmark star played more 398 games in all competitions and on almost half of his Premier League appearances kept clean sheets.

But it wasn't just his shot-stopping and handling that earned him a reputation as a big player. He was very vocal at shouting instructions – and sometimes abuse – at his team-mates in a bid to prevent goals!

Peter Boleslaw Schmeichel

Birthdate: November 8, 1963
Birthplace: Gladsaxe, Denmark
Position: Keeper
Clubs: Gladsaxe Hero, Hvidovre, Brondby, Manchester United, Sporting Portugal, Aston Villa, Manchester City
International: Denmark (129 caps, 1 goal)
Did you know? Peter scored a total of TEN goals during his career, six playing as a striker at his first club. Another came in the Premiership for Aston Villa against Everton and another was for Denmark.

MICHAEL LAUDRUP

A PLAY-MAKER and attacking midfielder, Michael Laudrup won four consecutive La Liga titles during his time with Barcelona.

He then moved to their main Spanish rivals Real Madrid and won a fifth title!

Laudrup captained Denmark 28 times and was voted the best Danish footballer of all time in 2006.

He missed his country's finest moment, when they won Euro 1992, as he'd had a row with the coach.

Michael Laudrup

Birthdate: June 15, 1964
Birthplace: Frederiksberg, Denmark
Position: Midfielder
Clubs: KB, Brondby, Juventus, Lazio (loan), Barcelona, Real Madrid, Vissel Kobe, Ajax
International: Denmark (104 caps, 37 goals)
Did you know? Michael and his younger brother Brian were both in FIFA's list of the 125 greatest living footballers. Their uncle Ebbe Skovdahl was manager of Aberdeen.

Super Swedes

HENRIK LARSSON

SEVEN MAGNIFICENT years at Celtic saw Henrik Larsson elevate himself to superstar status among the Bhoys faithful – and become a feared striker in the process. In his first season at Parkhead, the club won a Scottish Premier League and Cup double, ending a nine-year domination of the SPL by Rangers. Three more titles would follow, along with three more cups. He ended his career at Celtic Park with 242 goals in 315 appearances, and was named as Sweden's greatest footballer of the past 50 years. He hit 11 goals in 54 games to help Barcelona to two La Liga titles and a Spanish Supercup.

Henrik Edward Larsson

Birthdate: September 20, 1971
Birthplace: Helsingborg, Sweden
Position: Striker
Clubs: Hogaborgs, Helsingborgs, Feyenoord, Celtic, Barcelona, Helsingborgs, Man United (loan)
International: Sweden (101 caps, 37 goals)
Did you know? Larsson got a Premier League medal at Man United.

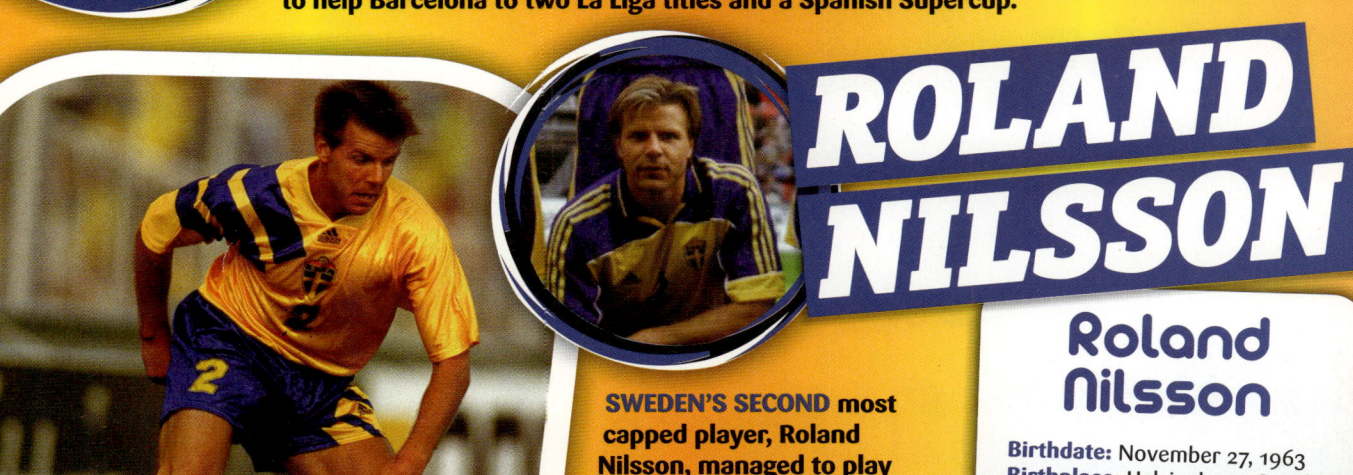

ROLAND NILSSON

SWEDEN'S SECOND most capped player, Roland Nilsson, managed to play top-flight football for more than 20 years. He earned cult status during his time in England with Sheffield Wednesday where fans reckon he was their best-ever right-back and best foreigner to play at Hillsborough. Nilsson also helped them into European competition for the first time in 30 years.

Roland Nilsson

Birthdate: November 27, 1963
Birthplace: Helsingborg, Sweden
Position: Defender
Clubs: Helsingborgs (three times), Goteborg, Sheffield Wednesday, Coventry (twice).
International: Sweden (116 caps, 2 goals)
Did you know? Nilsson was Sweden's Footballer of the Year in 1996, played his last tournament for them at Euro 2000, and became manager of Malmo in 2008.

SUPER SEVENS

KENNY DALGLISH

AS BOTH A PLAYER and manager Kenny Dalglish set records. But he will be best remembered as a skilful forward equally at home scoring goals or slicing open defences for his team-mates.

He was the first Scot to reach 100 caps and is still the country's joint top scorer on 30 goals with Denis Law.

Dalglish played 823 club games and scored 336 goals. He was a four times title winner in Scotland where he also won four Scottish Cups and a League Cup.

Dalglish's time at Liverpool was even more productive as he lifted three European Cups, six titles, four League Cups, an FA Cup, five Charity Shields and a European SuperCup.

Kenneth Mathieson Dalglish
Birthdate: March 4, 1951
Birthplace: Glasgow
Position: Forward
Clubs: Celtic, Liverpool
International: Scotland (102 caps, 30 goals)
Did you know? He is the only manager to win England's top flight with two different clubs: Division One with Liverpool, the Premiership with Blackburn.

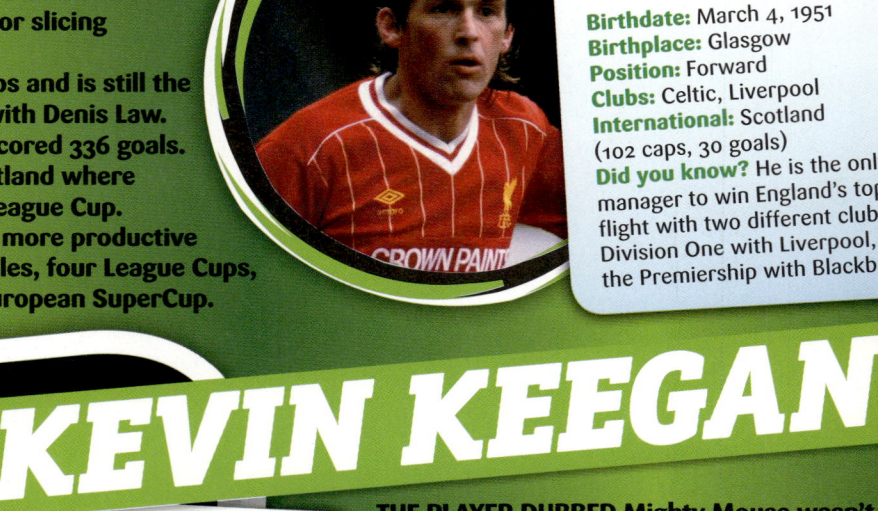

KEVIN KEEGAN

THE PLAYER DUBBED Mighty Mouse wasn't the most naturally gifted – but what he lacked in skill he more than made up for in passion.

Kevin Keegan suffered rejection and began his career in the old Fourth Division (League Two) before moving to Liverpool where he won three league titles, two FA Cups, two UEFA Cups and a European Cup.

A move to Hamburg saw him become European Footballer of the Year in 1978 and 1979. He returned to England with Southampton before dropping into Division Two (Championship) with Newcastle, who he helped to promotion.

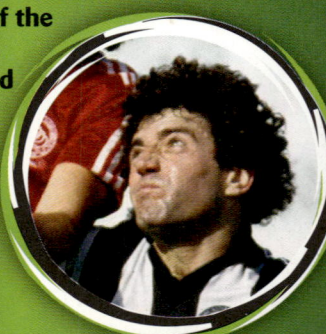

Joseph Kevin Keegan
Birthdate: February 14, 1951
Birthplace: Doncaster
Position: Striker
Clubs: Scunthorpe, Liverpool, Hamburg, Southampton, Newcastle United
International: England (63 caps, 21 goals)
Did you know? Special K learned how to speak German during his time with Hamburg and helped them to win their first title in 19 years.

NOTABLE NO.1s

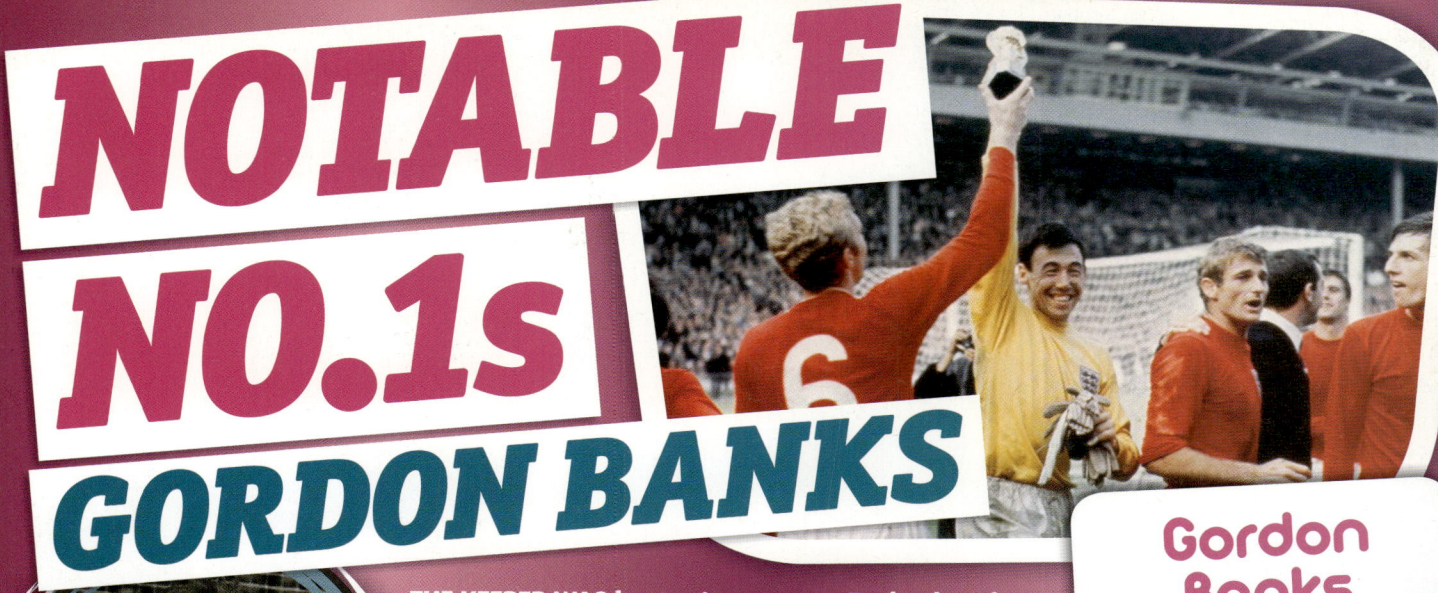

GORDON BANKS

THE KEEPER WAS beaten just once as England made their way to the 1966 World Cup Final at Wembley – and that was from the penalty spot!

Although he won that final, it was four years later that Banksy really made a name for himself at the 1970 finals in Mexico when he pulled off what was to be called "The save of the Century." This was a header from Pele that looked as though it was going in the bottom right hand corner of the goal until the keeper somehow managed to get a hand to it and flick the ball over the bar.

Gordon Banks
Birthdate: December 30, 1937
Birthplace: Sheffield
Position: Keeper
Clubs: Chesterfield, Leicester City
International: England (73 caps, 35 clean sheets)
Did you know? Banks lost the sight of his right eye in a car accident in 1972 shortly after being named Player of the Year.

PETER SHILTON

ENGLAND'S MOST-CAPPED player also took part in more than 1,000 league and cup games at club level. But it is his time under Brian Clough at Forest for which he is best remembered. Whilst at the City Ground Shilts won two European Cups, a league title, a League Cup and UEFA Super Cup. He was also named PFA Players' Player of the Year in 1978.

He played in three World Cups and two European Championships and set a joint record with former France keeper Fabien Barthez of keeping ten clean sheets in World Cup finals matches.

Peter Leslie Shilton
Birthdate: September 18, 1949
Birthplace: Leicester
Position: Keeper
Clubs: Leicester, Stoke, Nottingham Forest, Southampton, Derby, Plymouth, Bolton, Leyton Orient.
International: (125 caps)
Did you know? Shilts played more than 100 games for five different league clubs, a very rare occurrence.

GEORGE BEST

SIMPLY THE BEST

George Best

Birthdate: May 22, 1946
Birthplace: Belfast
Position: Forward
Clubs: Man United, Stockport, Cork Celtic, Los Angeles Aztecs (twice), Fulham, Fort Lauderdale Strikers, Hibs, San Jose Earthquakes, Bournemouth
International: Northern Ireland (37 caps, 9 goals)
Did you know? More than 100,000 mourners turned out for Besty's funeral in Belfast.

TWO YEARS STAND out in the life of George Best. The first was 1968 when he won the European Cup with Manchester United. The second was 2005 when he lost his life to a kidney infection at the age of 59.

Like his incredible footballing career, his life had come to a sad premature end.

Besty was the original rock and roll footballer, the "bad boy" whose life of high living and glamorous women didn't dampen his skills on the pitch.

He had fans on the edge of their seats watching amazing body swerves, shots and passes that David Beckham can still only dream about. The 1968 European Footballer of the Year also collected the English League titles in 1965 and 1967 and was the Football Writers' Footballer of the Year in 1968.

Yet his career total of 204 goals in 579 games plus all of the awards simply don't do justice to a player who many supporters still recognise as one of the best ever.

The talents of George Best are above comparison. Some players have tried to equal his skills, some may have come close, but there will only ever be one George Best!

WHAT THEY SAID...

Sir Bobby Charlton, former Manchester United team-mate: "Anyone who witnessed what George could do on the pitch wished they could do the same. He made an immense contribution to the game, and enriched the lives of everyone that saw him play."

Ingenius Italians

PAOLO DI CANIO

Paolo di Canio
Birthdate: July 9, 1968
Birthplace: Rome
Position: Striker
Clubs: Lazio, Ternana (loan), Juventus, Napoli, AC Milan, Celtic, Sheff Wed, West Ham, Charlton, Lazio, Cisco Roma
International: Nil
Did you know?
In 2000, di Canio was given a special fair play award after he caught the ball and refused to score because Everton keeper Paul Gerrard was on the ground injured and needed treatment.

THE ECCENTRIC BUT massively talented forward starred at Sheffield Wednesday, was a cult hero at West Ham and had an influence at Charlton before returning home for the latter stages of his career.

Having plyed his trade at a number of top clubs in Italy, England and with Celtic, many fans are still bemused at how di Canio never earned a call up by Italy. Hit the headlines when he was banned for 11 matches for pushing over a referee during his time at Sheff Wed.

PAOLO MALDINI

PAOLO MALDINI is the best defender Italy has ever produced. He is Italy's most capped star and the most selected for a team in the country's top-flight.

In these days of big money transfers he has remained loyal to AC Milan throughout his entire career. He began at the San Siro as a youth player in 1978 and is still part of their first-team squad 24 years after making his debut.

Among his many club successes are seven Serie A titles, five Champions League wins and five Italian Supercups.

Paolo Cesare Maldini
Birthdate: June 26, 1968
Birthplace: Milan
Position: Defender
Clubs: AC Milan
International: Italy (126 caps, 7 goals)
Did you know? Maldini was captain of Italy from 1994 to 2002, skippering the side a record 74 times.

ALESSANDRO DEL PIERO

ALTHOUGH HE PREFERS to play just behind the front striker, Del Piero has a good scoring record for club and country.

He joined Juventus in 1993, scored a hat-trick on his full debut and then fired goals to help them win their first title in eight years.

Del Piero has since won seven more titles, the Champions League and an Intercontinental Cup.

Great passing ability, good vision and the ability to perform like a midfielder have made him a valuable player to Juve who have struggled in his absence.

Alessandro Del Piero

Birthdate: November 9, 1974
Birthplace: Conegliano
Position: Striker
Clubs: Padova, Juventus
International: Italy (current)
Did you know? Del Piero is currently Juve's top appearance maker and record goalscorer. He scored one of the penalties that helped Italy lift the 2006 World Cup.

ROBERTO BAGGIO

Roberto Baggio

Birthdate: February 18, 1967
Birthplace: Caldogno
Position: Striker
Clubs: Vicenza, Fiorentina, Juventus, AC Milan, Bologna, Inter Milan, Brescia
International: Italy (55 caps, 27 goals)
Did you know? There were riots by Fiorentina fans when he was sold and more than 50 people were injured on the streets of Florence.

ROBERTO BAGGIO cost Juventus a then-world record fee of £7.7m when they bought him from Fiorentina in 1990, on the eve of the World Cup finals in his home country.

It proved to be money well spent as the already prolific goalscorer helped them win Serie A, the Italian Cup and UEFA Cup. He also became European and World Player of the Year in 1993.

An exceptionally gifted frontman, he became the first Italian ever to score at three World Cups, even though he missed a penalty in the 1994 final.

Magnificent Seven

EVEN THE BEST players in the world need someone to guide them. Here are some of Britain's best bosses over the years...

Brian Clough

An exceptionally gifted striker who played for Middlesbrough and Sunderland and whose career was tragically ended early by injury.

Teams managed: Hartlepool, Derby, Brighton, Leeds, Nottingham Forest.
Honours as a boss Derby: Division 2 (1986), Division 1 (1972) **Forest:** Division 2 promotion (1977), Division One (1978), League Cup (1978, 1979, 1989), European Cup (1979, 1980).
Remembered as... the best boss England never had! The people's choice as manager, but Cloughie wasn't the right man in the eyes of the Football Association.

Sir Bobby Robson

A midfielder with West Brom and Fulham, Sir Bobby made his name at Ipswich Town, where he won the UEFA Cup.

Teams managed: Fulham, Ipswich Town, England, PSV Eindhoven (twice), Sporting Lisbon, Porto, Barcelona, Newcastle United.
Honours as a boss Ipswich Town: Texaco Cup (1973), FA Cup (1978), UEFA Cup (1981). **England:** World Cup semi-finals, 1990. **PSV:** Dutch League (1991, 1992). **Porto:** Portuguese Cup (1994), Portuguese League (1995, 1996). **Barcelona:** Spanish Cup, Spanish Super Cup, European Cup Winner's Cup, European Manager of the Year (1997).
Remembered as... everyone's favourite grandad! He nearly reached the 1990 World Cup Final with England and they put up a statue of him at Portman Road.

Bill Shankly

The tough-talking Scot took no prisoners and his players knew they had to be willing to die for the cause. Set standards for others to follow.
Teams managed: Carlisle, Grimsby, Workington, Huddersfield, Liverpool
Honours as a boss Liverpool: Division 2 (1962), Division 1 (1964, 1966, 1973), FA Cup (1965, 1974), UEFA Cup (1973)
Remembered as... the man who made football's most famous statement: "Football is not a matter of life and death. It's much more important than that." And don't forget the Shankly gates at Anfield!

44

Bob Paisley

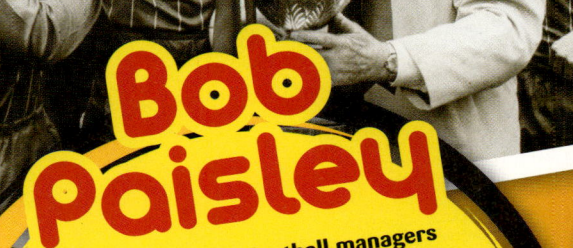

One of the greatest football managers of them all - the man who rose from being Liverpool's club physio and coach to collect a lorry load of silverware. An Anfield employee for 52 years!

Teams managed: Liverpool
Honours as a boss Division One (1976, 1977, 1979, 1980, 1982, 1983); UEFA Cup (1976); European Cup (1977, 1978, 1981); European Super Cup (1978); League Cup (1981, 1982, 1983); Charity Shield (1976, 1977, 1979, 1980, 1982)
Remembered as... the Durham miner's son who had to follow in Shankly's footsteps. Succeeded, and then some!

Sir Matt Busby

Another Scotsman who held the reigns at Old Trafford, even though he played for Manchester City and Liverpool. Twenty five years in charge but not as many games as Fergie.

Teams managed: Manchester United, Scotland.
Honours as a boss: Man United: Division One (1952, 1956, 1957, 1965, 1967); FA Cup (1948, 1963); European Cup (1968); Charity Shield (1952, 1956, 1957, 1965, 1967).
Remembered as... proof that there was life and success at Man United before Fergie. His memory lives on thanks to the road around the ground named after him.

Sir Alf Ramsey

No surprise that most fans only remember him for one thing (give you a clue...1966!). But he also had success at Ipswich and actually played 32 times as a defender for England.

Teams managed: Ipswich Town, England, Birmingham City
Honours as a boss England: World Cup (1966) **Ipswich:** Third Division South (1957); Division Two (1961); Division One (1962).
Remembered as... the only manager to win a World Cup with England. You can never take that away from him!

Sir Alex Ferguson

Created history by being the only man to win top-flight titles in England and Scotland. Has set new standards at Manchester United, his haul of silverware making him England's most successful manager ever.

Teams managed: East Stirling, St. Mirren, Aberdeen, Scotland, Man United
Honours as a boss St. Mirren: Scottish Division One (1977) **Aberdeen:** Scottish League (1980, 1984, 1985); Scottish Cup (1982, 1983, 1984, 1986); League Cup (1986); UEFA Cup Winners Cup (1983); UEFA Super Cup (1984). **Man United:** Premier League (1993, 1994, 1996, 1997, 1999, 2000, 2001, 2003, 2007, 2008); European Cup (1999, 2008); FA Cup (1990, 1994, 1996, 1999, 2004); League Cup (1992, 2006); Community Shield (1990, 1993, 1994, 1996, 1997, 2003, 2007, 2008); UEFA Cup Winners Cup (1991); UEFA Super Cup (1992); Intercontinental Cup (199)
Remembered as... the gaffer with the hairdryer who clobbered Beckham with a flying boot.

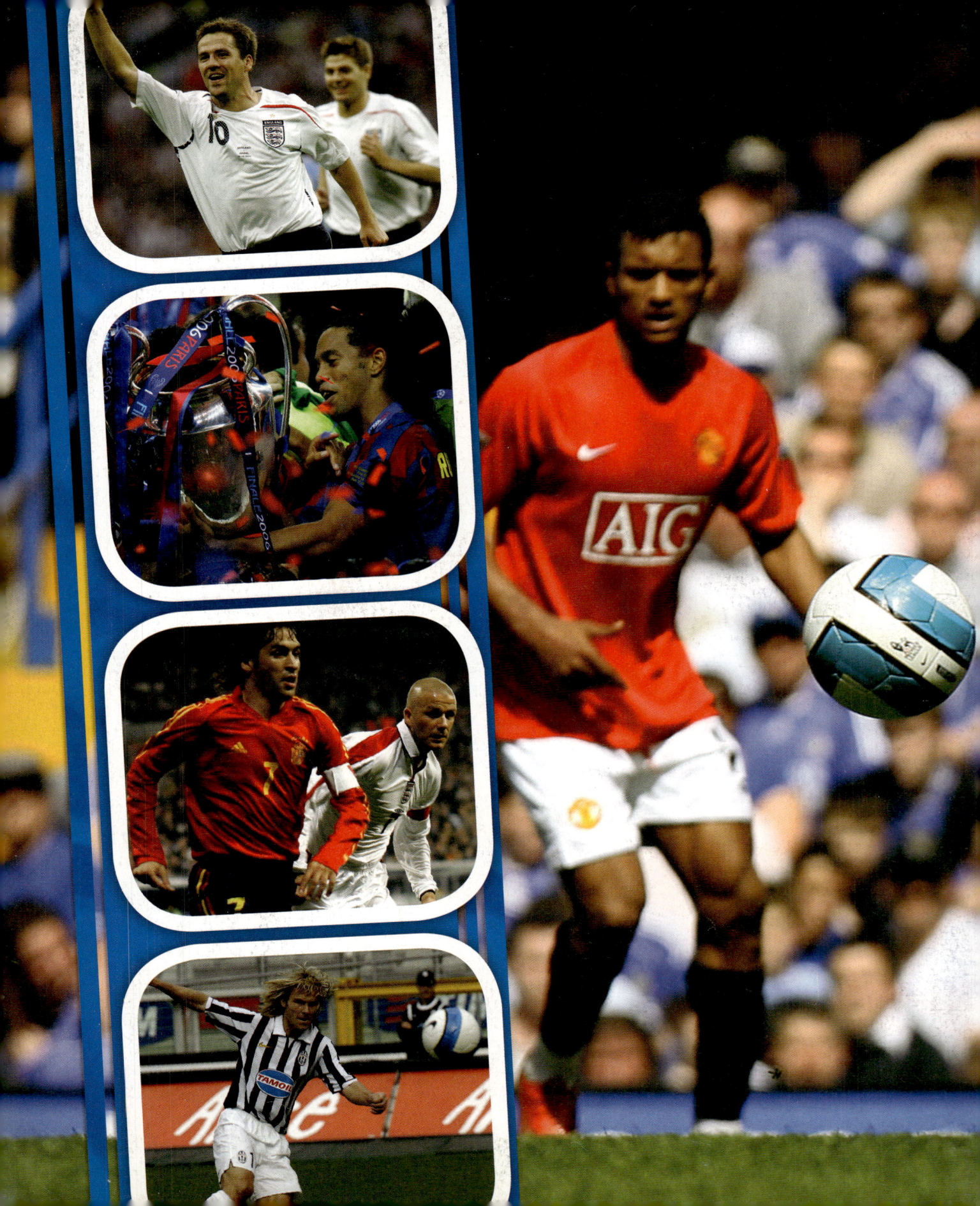